LIFE WITHOUT LIMITS

In Pursuit of Excellence

Morris J. Cerullo

"I find the great thing in this world, is not so much where we stand, but as in what direction we are moving."

Morris J. Cerullo

"¹As a prisoner for the Lord, then, I urge you to live a life worthy of the calling you have received. ² Be completely humble and gentle; be patient, bearing with one another in love. ³ Make every effort to keep the unity of the Spirit through the bond of peace. ⁴ There is one body and one Spirit, just as you were called to one hope when you were called; ⁵ one Lord, one faith, one baptism; ⁶ one God and Father of all, who is over all and through all and in all."

Ephesians 4:1-6

DEDICATION

It gives me great pleasure to dedicate this book to my Dad,
Pst Munga, My Mum and my three siblings; John Aggrey,
Juddy Becky and JoyAnn. Our stories, as a family has formed
the foundation of this great work.

To Dad and Mom,
For your generous support and insight;
The best teachers I ever have

Bro. John Aggrey,
For his selflessness will always be remembered.

Dr. Juddy and Sis. Joy,
For their endless support and encouragements.

My Nurse
Sister Grace Ontari
For your dedication and compassion that's unprescribed.

And

To
My dearest readers
Who are on their path to pursuing Excellence.

ACKNOWLEDGMENTS

It takes the work of many folks to get a book like this published. I'd like to thank the many people behind the scenes and across different organizations, that I don't get to interact with, but who work so hard to make this text a reality. Throughout the process, I was able to work firsthand with many great people who deserve acknowledgement.

Special gratitude to the Almighty God for granting me the knowledge, insight and making this book a success. Special acknowledgements to my wife and best friend for her unconditional love and prayers. The very best gift from the Almighty. A huge thank you to my family (parents and siblings) for all the support as I juggled various tasks while writing the book.

Much gratitude to:
Author Kenyatta Otieno, Pst. Lucas Mareva, Sister Ann Josephine and My Dad, for accepting to go through this manuscript to give it a better touch. God bless you so much.

All my mentors for the impact you all had in my life. May the Lord continue using you to impact more lives. Mr. Andrew Buop for your ever inspiring words and belief in me.

My brother and Co-founder of Lifespring Inspirations, Nelson Odhiambo Okuto. The journeys we have walked through the years have been fulfilling and have inspired me to write this piece of work. You always had my back and helped me work out through the book. God Bless.

Author John L. Mason, whose works have inspired me to get this manuscript done. His Books on "An Enemy Called Average" and "Conquering an Enemy Called Average" are the foundations of this wonderful piece. Pastor Alfred Arita of CITAM church Kapsabet, your work on the "A-Z secrets of High Achievers" been a great inspiration my brother. Keep on Inspiring lives.

And finally to my friends and everyone who accepted to be part of this great project.

Morris J. Cerullo

..

FOREWORD

I am delighted to write this foreword, not just in light of the fact that Morris Cerullo is a good friend, yet in addition because of my faith and belief in the quest and pursuit of excellence and the educative value of this book's discussion. My first definition of excellence was in the negative; excellence is not perfection. It took me time to rephrase that statement into; excellence is the pursuit of perfection even though practically nothing in life is perfect.

This book indeed provides a widely useful compilation of thoughts, ideas, and practical approaches to anyone who'd like to pursue excellence. Life without limits is a true reflection of our daily lives and a revelation of the fact that we all have the ability to rise and shine. This work is and will be an important resource to the present generation and the future generation. More so, it goes beyond demystifying the myths that pertain to excellence and beyond just making us aware of the seemingly underutilized learning settings with incredible but yet great stories of the author from childhood through his growth and upbringing .Africa is a continent full of talent which must pursue excellence to harness our individual and collective potential.

This book offers a variety concrete, useful and in-depth look at ways in which one can live a limitless life. It is a good book for teenagers and the youth as well as anybody in need of a refreshing punch.

Clearly written, well organized, and enormously practical, it should be part of every library.

Kenyatta Otieno
Author of Run Your Race

Morris J. Cerullo

CONTENTS

PREFACE

One forgets not and remembers the childhood memories and lectures that made him think, the friends that made him feel like he's part of a family, the nights that inspired stories of laughter and the late night lectures. Much more, one never forgets the messes, the "A" on the papers he spent all night writing, the adventures and the teams. These moments never end. They never vanish. The possibilities to achieve greatness are sure and continually infinite.

Life without limits is indeed a true life story, precisely penned down on such premise to inspire lives and bring hope of the ability of an individual to achieve excellence no matter the circumstances of life. This book recognizes and drives the fact that Success ain't generally an assurance; yet rather a phenomenon that one has to work through to accomplish. It isn't a certainty. More so, success and excellence are two terms thought to be synonymous despite the similarity in the language. While Success implies being the best, Excellence implies being at ones best. Whereas the former means being better than everyone else, the latter means being better tomorrow than you were yesterday. Success implies surpassing the accomplishments of other individuals. Excellence means matching ones practice with his potential."

The quest of excellence brings to play what life without limits entails. It originates from performing the best with what we hold to the glory of God and with the end goal of growth and improvement, yet not with a view to the score or who is watching from a man's point of view.

Scripturally speaking, the quest for excellence alludes to pursuing and getting along the best we can with the endowments and capacities given by God while giving our best to the resplendence of God. Ideally, in a perfect world it is performed without the aim of competition. This means tending to the common and routine issues, yet in extremely phenomenal ways while paying little respect to whether people are following or not. The reality is that; God sees our work and rewards us accordingly (1 Cor. 15:58).

It is my sincere belief that everyone got a story to tell. Life without limits perfectly explains my story which i'd like to use to demonstrate that anyone can rise to the occasion as long as he or she is psyched up to pursue excellence in whatever he or she does. Believe you me; excellence is not a reserve of the few, but for everyone who yearns for it.

A sneak preview of the book

From the beginning in the first chapter, the book goes a long way to describe where it all begun to the continuation of how one overcomes inertia in the second and third chapter while adopting a winning attitude in breaking the negative cycles. Moreover, it underscores the fact that being intentional in the sixth chapter drives one to rise above the crowd mentality in the seventh chapter while being on the move in the eighth chapter to go beyond the expectations of the ninth chapter. But most importantly, when all this is complete, then one has to read the tenth chapter to reposition him or herself to live above his circumstances as I do in the eleventh chapter. When all is said and done, your faith gets unraveled and you learn to let go the heavy burdens of the twelfth chapter while only giving glory to God by recognizing the power of prayer and living a life worthy of your calling as I do in the last chapter of this book.

"So think not what you see in the dirty rearview mirror as you drive away. Think about what you keep still in your heart and mind and look ahead, because you now beginning to dive into an enchanted and fascinating world and into a greater future. Awesome read."

Sir. Morris J. Cerullo

Morris J. Cerullo

.

CHAPTER 1
WHERE IT ALL BEGUN

"For the Lord Takes pleasure in his people; he adorns the humble with victory"
Psalms 149:4

Where it all begun..

B orn in the African continent and raised in one of the developing countries of the world, I indeed went through the same conditions that every young child undergoes. I witnessed every transformation in my life and in my country. Yet, in a world full of social, political and economic challenges and transformations that transcend geographical boundaries, one is commanded to stand out in excellence to achieve the best out of him.

True indeed, poverty ravages communities, good brains and personalities and reduces us to nothing. Despite the good learning institutions and rising living standards in regards to the studies conducted, the quest of excellence still remains a history and unattainable for a big population around the continent.

Born to a mother and father back in the early years, a young infant was taken to the fore of the world with large dreams and certainties. And despite, being Given birth to, in one of the middle income growing countries, this young child's parents' would still dream big despite the challenges of life then. My parents being believers and Christians would trust God for everything and they did so even before

I was given birth to. The faith they had was so big and when they trusted, the Lord never failed.

One surprising fact is that they had trusted God for children and even gave them names before conception. I really don't know how they knew the gender of their children before conception, but that's what I describe as walking in great and perfect faith. Then, there were no scanning machines to determine an infant's gender and even if there was, it would be expensive and useless to them, as they trusted God for this even before conception. They prayed and trusted God for these children. They would be called John Aggrey, Morris Cerullo and Juddy Rebecca Brown (Presently known as Dr. Becky Brown). Years later, we emerged as a fulfillment of their prayers. Even so, we grew up like any other child. As children, *"growing up in our motherland, Kenya, and residing in a small town called Awendo, for a number of years of our lives, created us a myriad of memories- some sad but most of them happy memories".* Living in a rental house in a community setup, we enjoyed an idyllic childhood within the safe and warm embrace of a loving family, good friends and a large and lovable extended family.

For a moment, I get to sit down with my siblings and parents and we get to realize how amazing it is, how we grow from careless kids to responsible teens. We question what really happens in the course of life that makes us responsible in our later years. Yet we realize that it's the seeds that we sow in the beginning that grows and becomes a huge tree, forming a canopy. As I sit here, silently thinking about my growth, enduring the changes, I wonder over some questions which seemingly don't have any answers, but I realize that it's because of such unanswerable situations that life has become a roller coaster ride.

As siblings, we grew up at a time when everyone treated each other like a Family. My siblings, friends and I went outside to play especially in the rain. Like any other child, we also had the opportunity to play in the mud and got dirty. Mum and dad punished us just like any other parent would do then. We played a variety of games unknown to the present day generation; hide and seek, bladder, three sticks, bano, and football. We ate

"It is the seeds that we sow in the beginning that grows and becomes a huge tree, forming a canopy."

different fruits; guavas, mangoes, and not forgetting the number of times we often walked barefooted! We had no PlayStations and neither did we play mobile games. Actually any parent who had a cellphone then became a call agent then if not the village superhero; most of them who basically happened to be teachers. We went hunting with 'feyaa' (catapult) and came back to roast the birds. Indeed, we weren't AFRAID OF ANYTHING. Life seemingly was good.

My elder brother, John Aggrey, became the sibling's lecturer at an early age. He taught me how to aim at birds using catapults and from the proceeds, we made soup from the birds. From him and his friends, Edgar, Fred Okello an Easton, we learnt how to make cars from wire-mesh and often had the neighbors fences being the victim as our raw materials and not our own fences. We actually underscored how important our fences were to us. We climbed trees and if one fell down, he would just get up and wait for next day to go pick money at that spot, and didn't tell our moms what happened! We challenged each other everywhere. If someone had a fight, that's what it really was... "A fight". Kids weren't afraid of fake guns when I grew up and neither were we afraid of water guns. We left our houses to the playground early in the morning or right after school till our parents or neighbors yelled out for their children as a reminder to get in the house for the night. If one kid was called for dinner, then we all knew it was time to go home. We rode our bikes, without helmets, through the alleys to secret places and sat around telling ghost stories. Actually, a friend's bicycle was communally owned and we all learnt how to share in whatever we had.

As a kid, I read a number of stories and played a number of childhood games. The experiences were diverse and taught us lots of creativity. We woke up to play using mud and we molded a number of things. Mothers were creative enough and often used a piece of white cloth and not funnels to distill water. During holidays, we visited the village to help graze cows, sheep's and donkeys. Life was well defined and everyone, including the children knew their roles.

I read numerous story books including bedtime stories. As a child I was made to believe that this story book was to be read while on bed and as soon as I began reading it, I fell asleep only to wake up the following morning. The childhood memories were just fascinating. We all went playing together, we swam at the rivers together fearlessly, watched over each other; and treated each other fairly. There was no favoritism. We had fun. We watched our mouths around our elders because we knew if we

DISRESPECTED any adult there would be a price to pay. Kids had manners and respected the old. Any parent would put you in place if you made a mistake.

Living under low incomes and occupations in a country which living standards were going up at a pace faster than the incomes, many were getting subjected to poverty. This was the case in our family but wasn't really going to be the defining moments of our lives.

Years passed by and in 1997, we moved to the lakeside town of Homa-Bay. Even here, life wasn't going to be so kind to us despite our kind stands. In our new home, we learnt how to make friends and move beyond the little problems life presented to us. Life was good and it was getting better. Yet even so, we still walked long distances to the lake occasionally over the weekend to even fetch water for our survival. This is what I had come to know as life as it was what was presented to us then. Good enough, no one had to be sorry for this. It was just life and what it presented to us.

Dad went to work in the morning and returned early enough to have time with his family. Mum had self-employed herself and was running some business. My elder brother as well had started schooling and both my parents did well to sustain the family. My mum made 'samosas' and sold them to fend for our family. Indeed two incomes are better than one; a fact that is not well understood by the present day generation.

Life wasn't really that easy and sure no one had assured us that it would always be a bed of roses. Cerullo was also joining school and so there was added responsibilities. Life had to go on.

Education wasn't going to be a choice but a right that has to be undertaken. That's was it and, my parent knew this. Living was by faith and indeed we trusted God. Time fled and at the right time, God came in. He declared according to his word in Jeremiah 29:11, "For I know the plans I have for you, says the Lord, plans for welfare and not evil, to give you a future and a hope." At this time, we really needed God to act and just as I was joining school, Mum was called in for a job at one of the organizations (name withheld). Having not applied for any job at the place, it was just God at work. Mum had sold 'Samosas' at the place sometime back and one of the bosses then had instructed the watchman at the gate to ensure the, 'woman' who comes selling samosas at the office is brought to his office.

Mum received the information and came to the office the following week as instructed. On her arrival, she was informed the officer had just driven out of office. This looked entirely lost and all that was left was just to walk out on the premises. Ephesians 1:12 says, "We who first hoped in Christ have been destined and appointed to live for the praise of his glory." This was the word. Mum walked out and just as she walked out, one of the vehicles was being driven out and to her surprise it was the officer who had been waiting to see her all along. It was so disappointing to the officer who felt that he had been lied to and duped by one of his employee.

God manifested himself then and mum was asked to report to work the following day. This was so surprising. Imagine being called to work that you haven't applied for- just because of good deeds..... This was the price she won for her dedications of pursuing excellence.

Pursuit of Excellence is really not a complex phenomenon as scholars may make it look like. Pursuit of Excellence simply means being at the best. To many, it may mean being better than others at a task; really No... excellence means being better today than you were yesterday and better tomorrow than you are today. Excellence means exceeding the other people's achievements. Excellence is never determined by comparing our score or performance against other people's scores and performance. The conditions may not be the same or rather the factors for your success and your friend's success isn't the same. The pursuit of excellence comes from doing our best with whatever we have to the give Glory and Honor of God the Father and with a view of improving and growing and not scoring.

Biblically, the quest of excellence entails pursuing and acting your best with the talents and abilities God gives you while committing your best to the Glory of God. In a nutshell, Excellence involves doing the common things by common people but in a very uncommon way, regardless of whether people are watching you or not. The realness is that God understands our work and rewards us accordingly just as stated in 1st Corinthians 15:58,

> *"The pursuit of excellence comes from doing our best with whatever we have to the Glory and Honor of God the Father."*

"Therefore, my dear brothers, stand firm. Let nothing move you. Always give yourself fully to the work of the Lord, because you know that your labor in the Lord is not in vain."

For sure he is a rewarder of those who believe in him.

CHAPTER NUGGETS

❖ It is the seeds that we sow in the beginning that grows and becomes a huge tree, forming a canopy.

❖ The quest of excellence entails pursuing and acting your best with the talents and abilities God gives you while committing your best to the Glory of God.

❖ Pursuit of Excellence is really not a complex phenomenon as scholars may make it look like. Pursuit of Excellence simply means being at the best.

CHAPTER 2
ALUTA CONTINUA

"Humble yourselves in the sight of the Lord, and
he shall lift you up. "
James 4:10

Aluta continua...

T he Lord watches over his people from his throne of Grace. Life without his Grace is a meaningless life and which can never achieve excellence. The Grace is however given to everyone in every measure and which sustains lives. There is a sure reason for everyone to live and excel despite the challenges and the only moment you stop living is the moment you die.

Childhood was one of the best moments in life. The days taught me to be creative, accept the life status and smile all the way regardless of the tough moments or sweet moments we underwent. Life continued and gave me always a reason to smile about. Family was always the basic unit of life support and happiness. The little moments it rained, it swept off the dust that was on the path and showers of blessings came over us just as the rain came over the land.

My siblings and I went to school; in fact, one of the best schools, then if not the best. School was always a friend and dad and mum did the best to cultivate this culture in all the siblings in the house. Even then, the weekends proved to be the best. Family time was just the best, fulfilling and awe-inspiring. Smiles all around made us strong. Dad and Mum were so strong and upbeat and taught us the same. ***Good behavior*** was instilled in us and ***morals*** founded our relationships. We lived in faith and trusted God. My siblings made the best moments out of every situation. Even as siblings, we occasionally put our strength to test but even in such moments we still afforded a smile after the fights.

Sincerely, the pursuit of excellence was not an excuse, but a force that we all had to reckon with. It was an ingredient, and an essential of life. Life was just sweet and got complimented by the actions we took at the moment to brighten our future. I recall the whole family walking to church every Sunday morning and back together after church. We all chatted and smiled our way back home despite the blistering sunlight. Having shaven during my school days, the sun was hitting me hard and often took a piece of cloth to cover my head .....The good old days were so good. We lived and embraced life as it presented itself and the future was always promising from our sight and not from others.

Years passed by and roles were calling. Mum had settled at her place of work and things were working to the Glory of God. God was working things out for us. My school performance was just awesome and so was performance of my other siblings. Dreams had been established. In the house was a pilot, a doctor and an engineer in the making. Despite all these dreams, it wasn't going to be an easygoing path to reach our aspirations.

The quest of excellence wasn't going to be a bed of roses and never has it been. Mom had moved some levels higher in her businesses and was an actual professional. She was just about to specialize but wait a bit; skills had to be passed to the other generations. The pursuit of excellence entails **passing on skills** at some point. Walking the walk entails the support of others. Mommy woke up as early as 4.00am to prepare her products. The rule of the business existed and everyone was aware from the old to the young in the house- "Late to bed, early to wake." We all slept late most of the times an hour to midnight. Mommy got to bed the latest and woke up the earliest. At about 4.00am mum was awake and 30 minutes later everyone was awake. Mum woke up to start preparation of some of the products as we helped and got to class to learn her skills. Trust me; this wasn't one of the best classes to attend then. Sleep was all over the eyes and it was attended under strict but close supervision.

"Aluta continua". This was the motto. And just like the Apostle Paul in Philippians 3:14, we totally had to press on till we attain what we desired. The cold was just not the

best one and not a friend to my elder brother who could fall ill due to his Asthmatic condition. We pressed on and encouraged ourselves. We sat by the fireplace outside the kitchen and got the heat from the fire. The Mandazis' were sweet and golden brown. We packed them into packets as mum cooked and illustrated her skills. Sure, one had to be keen as anyone of us would do it the next day, as our instructor watched. We learnt and passed the test. She became happy and impressed. And sincerely JoyAnn impressed the most having learned easily how to prepare all these products and become a jack of all trade- who she has become till date.

Surprisingly, everyone had to get into the kitchen and being a boy or male wasn't an excuse in my mother's school. Good for us today we do appreciate.

The morning came and the sky opened as we sat by the fireplace. Microwaves and ovens were unheard of and after the morning duty, we would all hurry to shower and cast on our uniforms. Breakfast was optional and nobody bothered even to prepare it. Sure, if it was there, it would be the hot black water. Work wasn't complete. This was only the start of a tough day ahead. We had to hasten to the various shops and do the supplies before rushing to school. We totally had to deliver our produce before being students at our schools.

We often got late and punished and really it became a normal thing. My morning prep at school would commence at 6.30am. At 6.00am, we would set off to the different shops in different locations to do the supply of mandazi's, cakes and crisps. We had become known suppliers including my parents. There was no apology to our business manager if you failed to do the supplies. This had become part of our family. To this end, we often paid the price of being late. But surely what would we do? It was indeed worth the sacrifice. Selling these products had paid our school

> **There was no apology to our business manager if you failed to do the supplies**

fees, rent and even other investments. Being late to do the supplies wasn't an excuse for being late to school and dad and mum were not to get this. Still, we afforded a smile and accepted our fate. Indeed we learned how to be responsible young men and appreciate the importance of work; a fact that most youths in the microwave generation attempt to shun at all cost.

The pursuit of excellence taught me a number of things:

1. Make no excuses

Most of us, including myself, in our pursuance of excellence, develop lots of excuses and tend to justify every reason why we fail to manage certain things in time. Pursuing excellence requires one to demystify every situation we experience that stops us from accomplishing all that is put before us. One thing that never rings loud in our ears is the fact that, the moment we begin to put excuses on our path to the pursuit of excellence, then we start putting limitations on our goals and abilities.

2. It involves sacrifices

Sacrifices are costly. They are expensive. Pursuit of excellence involves sacrificing a number of things, including those that one holds dear to him or her. Sacrificing our sleep wasn't the easiest task. Great achievements are never short of sacrifices. It is not until we sacrifice the things we hold dear to us that we achieve our goals and attain our destiny. Not sacrificing simply translates to us halting the achievements of our goals and postponing our destiny.

Life without limits involves one giving himself wholly to the course. The moment you stop doing so, then you begin to fail.

CHAPTER NUGGETS

- ❖ The pursuit of excellence is not an excuse, but a force that we all have to reckon with. It is an ingredient, an essential of life.

- ❖ In pursuing your best, then you must be willing to give yourself wholly to the course.

- ❖ The moment you begin to put excuses on your path to the pursuit of excellence, then you start putting limitations on your goals.

- ❖ Family is and will always be the basic unit of life support and happiness.

- ❖ Pursuit of excellence involves sacrifice

CHAPTER 3

OVERCOMING INERTIA

It is so hard to leave- until you leave. Even if you are on the right track, you'll get run over if you just sit there..."

Anonymous

Overcoming inertia

Pursuit of Excellence is a process and not a goal and so is living life without limits. Processes entail being on the move or continual action. That moment you begin to stall, then you are said to be at *inertia*. Inertia is the point at which, you are still and nothing seems to be working. Inertia is a force that everyone who is geared towards achieving excellence must reckon with. Really, there is no secret to overcoming inertia other than beginning at the point you are presently.

Progress just like success is not guaranteed if one cannot take initiative to start. For one to succeed in life, he has to decide to live a life that is defined by zero boundaries. He has to begin today and not tomorrow. He has to live a life without limits. Whereas the future seems bright, there is indeed no future in tomorrow if we can't take the initiative to work on our today. Today is indeed the right day to overcome inertia and begin whatever you can do. Begin now! Boldness has genius, power and magic in it. The future is determined by the present day actions and so is excellence.

Most of us are today at inertia and have become so comfortable with our levels. We have even become accustomed to the rules and let fear form the basis of our lives. One fact we ignore is the fact that at this position, we get so accustomed to the comforts of "I cannot", "I do not want to" and "it is too difficult" that we forget to realize when we stop doing things for ourselves and expect others to dance around us, we are not achieving greatness. We have made ourselves weak."

Life without limits is however not informed by living in a comfortable state. Yet the moment we become uncomfortable staying in this cocoon, then we get to a path of overcoming inertia and achieving excellence. Starting a business at a time when my mom wasn't employed, was the best way to overcome inertia and that drove her to getting a job. "Most times, the way isn't clear, but you want to start anyway. It is in starting with the first step that other steps become clearer."

The moment we realize the power that lies in beginning, then we get into the path to overcoming inertia and achieving excellence. Sure, opportunity is always where you are, never where you were. To get to any place, we must launch out for somewhere or else we get nowhere. Teddy Roosevelt remarks "do what you can with what you have, where you are." There is power in beginning. Utilize whatever you hold in your hand to begin the journey to your success today. Remember that opportunity knocks out once and that successful people accomplish more than any other, since they go ahead and do it before they are ready.

The truth is that, we can never know the much we can do till we try. One can never realize how much he can be a good cook unless he or she tries. One never realizes how much he can be a good writer, orator or even mentor till he tries. It's more honest to try than failing to try. The moment you fail trying, then you plan to fail. The most significant thing about achieving our dreams is starting right where we are. Edward Hail said," I cannot make out everything, but I nevertheless can do something; and because I cannot do everything, I will not refuse to do something I can do."

Until one is committed, there is: hesitancy, the chance & prospect to drawback, always ineffectiveness, concerning all acts of initiative and creation

Until one is committed, there is: hesitancy, the chance & prospect to drawback, always ineffectiveness, concerning all acts of initiative and creation. In that respect is an elementary truth in ignorance which kills countless ideas and splendid patterns. Commitment drives us to greater heights and makes our ideas and goals more effective.

To transform our nation, churches, schools, our families and dreams, then we got to begin today to be what we would like to become tomorrow. Most times we would always like to start the next day, next week or even after the holidays. With all honesty, there is no time like the present to get started. Begin now to be what you will be hereafter. You can cause this and become successful. Quit putting off what can be started today. Everyone procrastinates over time, however, this is determined by how much longer one wants to be in the condition or not?

Morris West once remarked," If you spend your whole life inside waiting for the storms, you will never enjoy the sunshine." Nobody touches the top without daring. Many people fail because they don't get started. They don't overcome inertia. They don't begin. We end up bringing a number of excuses that explains why things can't get done. We would become defensive and say, it was really hard or it wasn't the right time yet or there was simply too much right or the alarm didn't sound and so I overslept.

Nevertheless, a time comes when we got to put an end to the defensive responses to pursue a life that has no limits and excellence. Ernest Agyemang Yeboah says, "Kill your fear, and start something! God needs people for greater works, but fear always tells them how dangerous it is to take a step!" Our nation and professions need brave people who stand for what's right even in the wake of adversity and unjust rulers but fear always binds them and tells them how conformity is the only way to go. Our schools yearn for teachers and students who are able to stand their grounds and say 'NO' to impunity at the institutions, who would say 'NO' to exam cheating, yet fear reminds them that nothing is possible without the leakages and corruption at the institution. More importantly, our churches yearn for the leaders who would stand right and even talk against the social ills in the society, yet fear overcomes these leaders and reminds them how well they could live in such societies without even the fear of being held accountable or being judged.

We need to get to the point where we realize that every day is a new day to start over with a fresh outlook in life. Who will be in charge today? Is it the excuse or the powerful you?

> "Kill your fear, and start something! God needs people for greater works, but fear always tells them how dangerous it is to take a step!"
> — **Ernest Agyemang Yeboah**

If the alarm didn't go off, admit that you didn't set it properly, and for almost every reason, when something does not happen, then there is a reason that it could happen.

To live a life without limits, we got to keep little excuses from becoming big excuses. We need to take small steps to increase our success in life and begin today. And really, what do we have to do? What will you do?

> Will you start being more of who you are?
> Will you begin improving your relationship?
> Will you start improving yourself?
> Will you begin today? When will you begin?

Jeff Olson the author of 'The slight edge' says, "The sweat to success starts with your philosophy. It doesn't take a lot; it just takes a little each day to reshape the results you are getting. It takes practice to get better. "What's your philosophy?

Epicurus said, "Do not spoil what you have by desiring what you have not; but remember that what you now have, was once among the things you hoped for." Henry Amiel observed, "Almost everything comes from nothing." Therefore, we have to begin with that which we have in our hands at the moment.

CHAPTER NUGGETS

- ❖ Pursuit of Excellence is a process and not a goal.

- ❖ Every day is a new day to start over with a fresh outlook in life.

- ❖ There is sure no future in tomorrow if you can't work on your today. Today is the right day to overcome inertia

- ❖ Until one is committed, there is: hesitancy, the chance & prospect to drawback, always ineffectiveness, concerning all acts of initiative and creation.

- ❖ "It takes practice to get better"
- ❖ It is in starting with the first step that other steps become clearer."

CHAPTER 4

A WINNING ATTITUDE

*"Desire is the key to motivation, but its determination
and commitment to an unrelenting pursuit of your goal -
a commitment to excellence - that will enable you to
attain the success you seek."*
Mario Andretti

Role of attitude in pursuit of excellence

Richard Bach says," sooner or later, those who win are those who think they can." Pursuing excellence is a game-plan that begins from the mind and is defined by a person's attitude- that inward feeling towards something or someone that is expressed outwardly.

While at class five (otherwise known as grade V by the group of schools attendees), I was blessed to have been learning at a private institution together with my siblings. Thank God we had strict instructors and parents who not only monitored our performance but as well went through our books without tiring at all. By God's grace, my siblings and I were doing well and we topped our classes. God's favour was sure resting upon our lives. We literally perfomed well in every category.

Interestingly, during these days, performance was gauged on one's ability to attain the highest mark and failure to hit the pass mark would always result into a punishment. Being top student, excellence was expected of you. Scoring ell in all the subjects except one amounted to one being regarded as a joker, if such a term ever exists. I seemingly was such a pupil; scoring the highest possible mark in mathematics and slightly below the pass mark belt in one of the other subject. Our teachers' then would absolutely make good use of the biblical verse, "spare the rod, spoil the child."

Actually, having a double lesson in that subject would just prove the worst day of the week. The day just became boring as pupils below the pass mark belt, would be at the mercy of the teacher. We tried reading and reading even into moments just before our exam papers, but the performance wasn't pleasing to our teacher. Funny enough, the number of tests the teacher gave were just too much. We sat the papers weekly and for a moment, we thought the teacher would just enjoy punishing us. Could be this was the case. Who knows? Only God and him.

Unfortunately things never changed on my end and even got worse in the following years. I often became a victim of my teacher's wrath. I for sure had something wrong with me, scoring highly in the rest of the subject, but just below the belt in this specific subject. While in this class, I thought the rivalry between me and the teacher had grown and had to act.

I couldn't take it anymore. I wasn't going to allow myself get punished over and over. I couldn't achieve the teacher's pass mark of attaining ninety nine percent in the subject. It was just unimaginable. I became smarter and concocted a plan.

Indeed, one never misses an idea. On the closing day, I walked home and presented my report form to dad as it was the norm. I had attained the second position in our class despite my poor performance in this one subject. Dad would absolutely question my performance in this subject. As soon as he did, I took it in and honestly informed him of my intentions of not going back to that school. The look that came from his face, communicated everything. Maybe you could understand this.

I became decisive as he is and unmoved by his facial expressions, I went on with my plan. I took my lunch and quietly walked out of the house to a nearby school just a kilometer away. I had desired to study at this school since my primary two. This was a special opportunity indeed. It had for sure presented itself and was ready to seize it. One fact is that, *"lifetime opportunities are seized during the lifespan of that opportunity."*

A go-getter I was and have been to date. I courageously walked through the school gate to the Head teachers' office and presented my plea. My academic report form spoke on

> **"Lifetime opportunities are seized during the lifespan of that opportunity."**

my behalf. The headteacher was very impressed and asked me to tag along with my parent the following day.

I walked back gladly and smiled all the way, despite not knowing the reception I would receive back at home. My plan had succeeded temporarily. The building at my new school had just fascinated me. I absolutely loved the place. I fell in love with the uniform; I fell in love with everything about it. I was so upbeat about it and felt like the schools would open tomorrow. My attitude about the school was simply honest. Meanwhile, at home, dad and mom were waiting for me. I surprised all of them when I informed them they were needed at school the following day for my intake. The next day, I walked into the school with my dad and the head teacher was so kind to give me a cup of porridge. Indeed nothing deters a determined soul.

Life seemed pretty good right now. The head teacher was impressed and informed my dad of my intake. At this moment I felt like my problem had been solved now that I had flown away from that school. Opening day came and I reported. Exams came and I did them. Unfortunately, my problem with this subject, remained unsettled. I still performed under the belt. For sure, the school wasn't the reason for my failure but something much more within myself. I just recount the feeling; quite a shitty one. Indeed no matter how much fault we find we another, and regardless of how much we blame them, that doesn't hange us.

I did my final Primary Education exams and joined a high school, though not of my choice. Life wasn't any better here. The number of subjects had increased. It was in this level that I came to realize my problem. My performance required a change of tact. I was getting into my final year and this is when I had a meeting with myself and discovered the secret. Though late, it wasn't too late for me. I had discovered the secret. The secret was developing a right attitude towards the subject. I performed in the subject in my final national examinations and secured a chance to join a university. To me this was excellence.

The developments I went through, brought to my realization yet another ingredient of living a life without limits in my pursuit of excellence; - ***Developing a different thinking and perspective of the common things.***

Friends, present day generations fancy being part of the majority. Conformity has taken over our children, youths and couples. Living a life without limits entails being a candidate of change and the ability to stand out and think differently from the majority. Indeed, for a long while, I was part of the majority who thought certain subjects were difficult and a reserve for the few who excelled in them. But the moment I began being a candidate of change after more than four years, I began to excel. When you begin to think and see things differently as opposed to the majority, then you begin to see an outstanding result and change.

Pursuing excellence requires of us to act on our attitude an keep it positive always. One can never underestimate the value of having the right attitude in life. Life is all about attitude and which determines the far one can go and achieve. And just like my pastor says, an attitude has the power to affect one's performance, positively or negatively. He states, "Negative attitude, leads to poor performance, and those who set low targets, achieve low."

> **When you begin to think and see things differently as opposed to the majority, then you begin seeing an outstanding result and change.**

Positivity is all. What one thinks of himself is all that he becomes. Think success, not failure. Beware of negative environments around you, and know that the moment you say to yourself, "I CANNOT," then you won't. In all that you do, remember positive things happen to positive people, and simply as negative things happen to negative people. Indeed, with a right attitude, you don't give up, however, terrible things may be.

This is the only key to pursuing excellence that enables you overcome whatever you hear and whatever you see. I so suggest, that this central, right attitude, be part of you forever, whenever you are in a race to your destiny...

How can one build up the quest for excellence? What are a portion of the things required by way of the means of pursuing excellence?

From the point of view of that which influences the manner in which we work, there is presumably nothing more imperative than one's attitude! Our attitude impacts each and every choice we make on an everyday, minute by-minute premise. It either fires our expectations and the quest for the things that are vital or it extinguishes our expectations and interests. The estimation of one's demeanor on what we seek after—our qualities, needs, targets, and how we seek after them is exceptionally obvious in the book of Philippians where one of the topics is that of bliss or rejoicing in the Lord regardless of what the circumstances or conditions of life.

Having a right attitude indeed plays a big role in ensuring one lives a life without limits in the pursuit of excellence. The moment one changes the way they look at things, the things one perceives changes to the positive.

> *"Always have a positive attitude in life. There is something always positive in every person. Even a stopped watch is right twice a day!!!"*

<u>CHAPTER NUGGETS</u>

❖ Developing a different thinking and perspective of the common things is an ingredient of pursuit of excellence

❖ When you begin to think and see things differently as opposed to the majority, then you begin seeing an outstanding result and change.

❖ To pursue excellence, you have to act on your attitude and keep it positive always.

CHAPTER 5

BREAKING THE NEGATIVE CYCLES

"Your chaotic present is someone else's nostalgic past."

Breaking the negative cycles

J ust like habit is a story defining what we've done before, what we doing right now and what we are planning to do in the future, so is a negative cycle a story telling of negativity. It's easier to be entrapped by a cycle of negativity. Negative thoughts and energy, just like positive thoughts and energy, are literally contagious and propagate themselves. Yet there is a possibility of transforming any cycle of negativity into a positive one by making a deliberate choice to do so and intently focusing on it.

One fact is that we have all been there at a time. Getting trapped in situations that suck. During this moment, everything sucks. The people around suck, the day sucks, the weather and everyone we meet sucks. There is nothing that seems great. Nothing even seems to be on the TV as the TV programs also suck. Life comes to a halt. It stops being fun. The slightest things provoke us and even turn into fodder for an angry rant. Its for sure a shitty feeling that runs around us.

One thing is that the moment one finds himself in such a feeling, then he is seemingly just at the middle ground of a negativity cycle. It's not easy, but this can be turned around. One of the worst thing, however, could be walking with a failure or rejected tag within oneself. What a suicidal moment!

My story in the previous chapter is a vivid example of one who's trapped in negative cycles. The failure to perform often makes us feel that we are failures and consequently affects our relationships. Interestingly the cycle of negativity starts from our thoughts that become words, then actions, habits, character and which finally becomes our destiny.

Most people entrapped in the cycle of negativity are not short of this cycle. Once one is trapped, then it takes great dedication to walk out of the cycle. Our connections are critical to helping us walk in to and or out of such cycles. One great personality who helped me walk out of my negative cycle was my high school desk mate and close friend, Nelson Okuto. His words of encouragement resulted to a change of attitude in my life and which prompted an improvement in my performance. Attitude is really an important facet of

> *Never walk with the 'failure' or 'rejected' tags...*

breaking negativity. Ideally, nothing good is able to stand without the **right attitude**. One may know how to do this, but if the **attitude** is **negative**, all one can say is "I could have done it." There is indeed too much **negativity** in the world but which we should not contribute to.

From my accounts of life stories, the moment I took *radical responsibility* for my mood and choices, I found *incredible freedom.* I stopped blaming others around me for my negativity and started looking inward. I remembered that everything I see and experience is a reflection of my inner self, and I understood that no outside thing was causing me pain, there was no "cycle"- only my story of it, and there was only one way to feel better – through an internal change.

This is so helpful! We may be new to this way of thinking that we can take responsibility for our own happiness, and that orientating our minds to habitual positive/constructive thinking is really more of a choice than anything else. Personally, I have since developed a radical gratitude list which I sure cherish so much. My body, my life and today are things I'm always grateful for.

The Trap of Negative Thinking

What's A Negativity Cycle?

I have spoken much concerning the trap of negatve cycle. It's quite unfortunate that we often find ourselves in negative cycles without even realizing. And whereas the Cycle of Negativity may sound like a really fancy-pants name for being in a bad mood; and probably it kind of is. Yet while a bad mood can come and go, a negativity cycle is a spiral in which an individual basically becomes addicted to negativity.

To snap out of the cycle, one has to;

i.   Identify the negative thinking

Identification is always the first step towards any problem solving. Identifying your negative thoughts is the first step towards letting it go. It needs self-reflection and quiet moments with oneself to demystify the negativity one has within him or herself.

This is a tough situation to escape because it's self-perpetuating, as anyone stuck in negative thinking knows all too well. Negative experiences feed your negative expectations, which then attract new negative experiences.

ii. Realize we're in it

Usually negative patterns and cycles are pretty huge and uncomfortable. Ranging from being in terrible jobs, to allowing yourself be treated in undesirable ways, to inadvertently attracting the wrong type of romantic partner, negative patterns and cycles are pretty painful. Despite these, the good news is, cycles and patterns can absolutely be broken (if you want them to). The secret is to become aware that a pattern exists, and to understand how and why you are creating that pattern. The first step to breaking a negative cycle is to realize we're in it- and that we're telling a story of that cycle, which reinforces it.

iii. Intense self-reflection

Once we realize we're telling a story of the negativity cycle, then we need to begin the process of recovery. Making peace with oneself and with your pattern by intense self-reflection in whatever form you're drawn to – through spiritual development, therapy, energy healing, meditation, or any other form of deep inner work. As you know, a myriad of all kinds of therapies are available, and only you know best what will help you at certain times in your life.

Once you break a cycle or pattern, for the most part it will be DONE, however, I've noticed that sometimes residual energy will show up, kind of like a blip on a radar, before it becomes obsolete. And if you find that does happen, you can also do more work and reflection to clear that up, too.

With experience in healing process, one doesn't often just focus on the problem or issue once and heals forever. It is a process and, just like you don't go to the gym one time and lift weights and expect lasting results. Inner work takes focus, determination, and dedication – but the results are beyond worth it.

CHAPTER NUGGETS

- ❖ Negative thoughts and energy, just like positive thoughts and energy, are literally contagious and propagate themselves.

- ❖ we can take responsibility for our own happiness

- ❖ The first step to breaking a negative cycle is to realize we're in it

- ❖ Identifying your negative thoughts is the first step towards letting it go.

CHAPTER 6

BEING INTENTIONAL

"But above all, my brothers, do not swear, either by heaven or by earth or by any other oath, but let your "yes" be yes and your "no" be no, so that you may not fall under condemnation. James 5:12 ESV "

Being intentional

No purpose, No direction, No achievement. Greater achievements start with actions done intentionally. You certainly not going to sit down and relax and hope things gonna work out....Hell No....you got to work it out. Intentional living is part of human life; whether a Christian or not. Being intentional is understanding the reason as to why you got to do something, making a decision to do it and planning on how to get it done. Get me right friends. I am not saying that it is wrong to be spontaneous. There's nothing wrong with being spontaneous.....I am at times and so are my siblings. Actually there are number of times my siblings and I would wake up and hit the road for a road trip or even just come up with a plan after lunch or dinner and get rolling. However, in as much as it's good to be spontaneous at times, our calling is to be purposeful.

> "There's nothing wrong with being spontaneous. However, in as much as it's good to be spontaneous at times, our calling is to be purposeful."

Beginning this year and beyond...we got to decide to be intentional in everything we do. We just can't afford to fold our hands, cross our legs and just let things pass by hoping someone else would act and we'd follow. And just like Mahershala Ali says, "You have the capacity to leave a lasting impact and indelible impression upon this world....Claim the sacred spaces of your minds, nurture and cultivate a vision of fulfillment, and move toward that destiny with patience, perseverance, and prayer." God really cares about what you going to do today, tomorrow and the rest of the year. He wants us to be intentional. No one finishes well by accident.

Wondering whether we all have met this one friend who is ever open to everything and anything.... whenever he's asked out, he's always ready. Being intentional is about what your true values are, then making deliberate choices to prioritize these values. True indeed, unintentional life accepts everything and does nothing. An intentional life embraces only the things that will add to the mission of significance. You got to be intentional and live your story the best way. One of my best Author's, John C. Maxwell, says, "When you live each day with intentionality, there's almost no limit to what you can do. You can transform yourself, your family, your community, and your nation. When enough people do that, they can change the world. When you intentionally use your everyday life to bring about positive change in the lives of others, you begin to live a life that matters."

Being intentional is a choice. Realize that every morning is a new day full of decisions and opportunity. You get to pick your attitude and your decisions. Evaluate the culture that you're swimming in. Life is not lived in a vacuum. It can never be your dress your choice or even something close to that. You got to examine yourself and know who you are. Develop your yearly plans and goals and act towards these plans. Living a life that's limitless in the pursuit of excellence, requires us to be intentional. It requires us to be decisive in all we do. The moment you have broken the negative cycles, all you need is to become intentional in what you do. This allows you to rise above the crowd mentality and get on the move.

Being intentional goes beyond just what we think. It goes beyond the normal perspectives of life. It changes our perspective about issues. More so, when I started becoming intentional, I realized that problems are the price of our progress. Living the limitless life entails looking at our obstacles of life from a different angle. When you begin being intentional, you

> *Life is not lived in a vacuum. Examine yourself. Know who you are.*

begin to realize that obstacles of life are intended to make us furnished and move us up the ladder to the next level. Oral Roberts, a preacher, says that, "you cannot bring about renewal or change without confrontations." It is true that things never come on a silver platter but how about if we began looking at things from an intentional perspective? Probably when we begin doing so, we would be like Scott Alexander who remarks that problems are a sign of progress. It is a sign that wheels are turning. One true fact is that the present day adversaries and obstacles are the best price we got to pay for tomorrow's accomplishments. Come on. Be intentional like David was. He chose to face the Israelites obstacles. He viewed Goliath as a too big obstacle to miss.

Precautions to take while being intentional

1. Don't burn bridges

The importance of a bridge is only known to one who uses the bridge. A number of us never realize how important the bridges are till we find ourselves at the river bank. Come on! The contractor wasn't mad to design the bridges at certain points. Most importantly, he never just woke up and decided that the bridge has to be at that point. Woe unto you if you destroy the bridge. When the rains come, you'll get to know the purpose of the bridge you destroyed.

In as much as I'm giving a wake up call to each one of us to become intentional in this year going forward, I'm critical of the fact that in most cases we need to cross to the other side by the use of the bridge. We live in such a small world that it's critical not to burn bridges. One thing is that you ain't going to like everyone and neither are they going to like you. Sincerely how would it even be if you'd be loved by everyone? What would the world be like? Where would the individuality of self arise from? And where would the uniqueness of relationships be? It would be non-existent.. The concept of attraction, desire and love would literally be nothing.

Enough of this. If we are going to be intentional, we still got to embrace other divergent personalities and views. It is the desire of every individual to get stronger and more confident. We ain't going to be intentional by forgetting the bridges we went through. I'm sorry if you thought that's the case. We ain't going to be intentional by just being unethical to those who let us get to our positions. In as much as we going to be intentional by focusing on our own path, we got to realize the power of walking through the path with others. No matter what you do, certain people will like you and others would not. Your goal in this journey of intentional living would be to find the people who resonate well at your frequency. And not to placate and appease the over five billion personalities globally.

2. Take risks

Being intentional is a decision one is going to make. When I was young, I learnt from my dad, an aspect in risk taking. I learnt that life is all about risking. Did you ever know that our life revolves around risk taking? Eating is a risk. One may get chocked. Walking is a risk. One may get knocked down. Cooking is a risk. One may get burned. Intentional living is not any different. It is a risk.

Life is indeed full of ups and downs. However, we can't let ourselves fizzle out in unhappy situations. We can't go down certain paths because it's what someone else would desire for us. No! It is imperative that we strive for our own goals and happiness. Oftentimes, it is the risks and chances we abscond that we regret the most. If we going to be intentional, then we got to take risks.

3. Don't just become a Dinosaur

This is quite interesting. I'm certain we have watched a number of movies with images of dinosaurs. I find them scary and I know you do as well in as much as you wouldn't admit. Enough of that. A number of us often believe that the moment you make a decision to be intentional then you got to stop listening at the words of other people. That's your own thinking. Just because you decided to be intentional doesn't make other people's arguments stupid. Just because you decided to be intentional doesn't mean you stop learning. You got to read and read and read. If you don't keep old skills sharp and continue learning new ones, you begin becoming obsolete instead of being intentional. That's quite sad and annoying.

Don't shy away from the leap of being intentional. You can make it.

CHAPTER NUGGETS

- ❖ Negative thoughts and energy, just like positive thoughts and energy, are literally

- ❖ Intentional living is part of human life; whether a Christian or not.

- ❖ Present day adversaries and obstacles are the best price we got to pay for tomorrow's accomplishments.

- ❖ If we are going to be intentional, we still got to embrace other divergent personalities and views.

Morris J. Cerullo

CHAPTER 7

RISING ABOVE THE CROWD MENTALITY

"Be a yardstick of quality. Some people aren't used to an environment where excellence is expected."

Steve Jobs

Rising above the crowd mentality

The title alone may lead you to believe this is going to be a chapter that encourages you to be unconventional for the sake of being unconventional. That builds up to telling you the secret sauce to a life of success is as simple as just doing the opposite of everyone else.

Well, it's not that chapter as you think. But if you want such type of material, the web is full of examples, good and bad, and I bid you a fond farewell.

What this chapter entails, is an invitation; an invitation to celebrate and, if necessary, reclaim your ability to think independently. This chapter is indeed an invitation to celebrate having a slightly different view of the world if that's you. Finally, it's an invitation to reconnect with your own inner spark.

Alexander Hamilton says, "There is a certain enthusiasm in liberty that makes human nature rise above itself, in acts of bravery and heroism." Mike Huckabee as well quotes, "It's when ordinary people rise above the expectations and seize the opportunity that milestones truly are reached."

These two quotes from the two personalities inform my desire to keep going despite the crowd mentality.

Joining the university during my years seemed fashioned and was a sign of success and excellence. The community indeed held you with a high regard and for sure, you became the hope of the family' and not only the family but the community at large. In high school, the teachers gave their experiences as they taught as well the visiting university students and alumni's. The experiences seemed awesome and cool and we all longed to be there and so we worked smart with an ultimate goal of joining the university to live such kind of a life. From their words, it looked like a roller coaster. Life in accordance to their experiences wasn't as strict as it was currently then in high school; reading was optional and sleep was too. It was a matter of choice and relationships formed the base of their lives at the institutions of higher learning.

Time came and we all joined different universities in the country. Unfortunately, in my case, I opted to do a different course than that which I had been called to do and so I changed to a private university. Being alone from my previous school, I had to make friends as fast as I could. At the institution, I met people from different backgrounds, different faiths, different value systems and both male and female gender and probably there could be a transgender too. I had hoped life would be as easy as the tales we had before but really was it really going to be so... time would tell.

I made friends so quick and fortunately in the process met my former school mates. By the time the second semester was nearing an end; I had made a number of friends and dropped some. I remember one day after the lectures, I went to a party with my friends from school. My parents had brought me up in a respectable and honorable way and mom had always told me not to allow myself be a victim of peer pressure. Partying was again never my thing but due to friendship, I couldn't miss joining my friends this time and so I went to make a casual appearance just as it was my habit. All my friends were enjoying the party except for me who was struggling to cope up and one of my friends (name withheld) noticed this. I had never got to a place where there was a drinking spree before like this. A number of my friends were getting drunk and some new members were being won.

The trap had been set and they had contemplated to have me join the spree as well and at some point. In self-defense, I declared my stand and unfortunately walked out of the party after a while. The drinking spree had got so many friends of mine influenced to join the drinking den. Peer pressure had forced a couple of others to do what they hadn't been doing and this is what I refer to as the ***crowd mentality.***

The dictionary refers to the *crowd mentality* to be synonymous to *Herd mentality*, or *mob mentality*. The terms, describes how people are influenced by their peers to adopt certain behaviors.

Today, most of us have fallen victims to the crowd mentality both knowingly and unknowingly. For instance if you ask the youths there reasons for joining the social media pages like Facebook and Instagram, most of them are influenced by the crowd and their peers. For sure, as adults it's so easy to become socially conditioned. Socially conditioned to accept the theories of others as fact. To accept second-hand ideals and second-hand information and absorb it all as if it was in fact our own. Actually, most parents fail not to realize how their own offspring's find themselves in such situations.

Moving in a crowd has its benefits of course. It makes us feel safe. It makes us feel part of the gang. But what if being in the herd is not really for us at all?

Walk your own path

Perhaps instead we choose to tread our own path.

What if we stopped considering others to grant us all the answers but yet focused on our own self? What if we looked at the horizon and felt a sense of wonder and adventure?

What if we set our inner compasses on a journey of our own making? And what if we aligned our actions and priorities with what's really important to us?

What if we committed to really seeking our own paths? To learning from others but staying true to ourselves along the way. Staying true to who we want to be. Committing to seek and appreciate all the goodness along the way.

Isn't all of that worth separating from the crowd from?

Overcoming the crowd mentality is something that a number of us have found it difficult to contend with especially the youths in the current century. Mark Twain observes, "Whenever you find yourself on the side of the majority, it is time to pause and reflect."

The desire to walk my own path has always resided within myself. I hope this isn't misquoted as being egocentric. One thing I believe is that we need others to help us attain excellence. It is a collective endeavor but even as much as we need others to help us through achieve success, we have the biggest role to play. There are journeys that you have to take alone and as much as you need others at some point of the journey, you have to realize that everyone has his own path just like in athletics; every athlete has his line to run in or else risk getting disqualified. The truth is in as much we may run the race together with others; every individual runs his own race.

One thing that is that chatting your own path is never easy. Opposition comes even from unexpected quotas; from the family, the church and friends. Most importantly, there is need to always stand for the right and stop any attempt to fall prey to the crowd mentality. One thing that I learnt from my childhood and parents is the fact that we all got to stand for the right things. It matters not what people are going to say. It matter not what if people are going to disown you, what is right is ever right and that which is wrong is always wrong.

The moment we understand these important aspect of life then overcoming the crowd mentality is always inevitable.

*"Remember, everyone has their own path. Walk yours with integrity and wish all others peace on their journey. When your paths merge, rejoice for their presence in your life. When the paths are separated, return to the wholeness of yourself. Give thanks for the footprints left on your soul, and embrace the time to journey on your own...break free from the **crowd mentality** and Excellence is guaranteed."*

CHAPTER NUGGETS

❖ Most of us fall victims to the crowd mentality both knowingly and unknowingly.

❖ Moving in a crowd has its benefits of course. It makes us feel safe. It makes us feel part of the gang. But what if being in the herd is not really for us at all?

❖ In as much we may run the race together with others, every individual runs his own race.

* * * *

CHAPTER 8

BE ON THE MOVE

*To me, if life boils down to one thing, it's movement. To
live is to keep moving.*
Jerry Seinfeld

Be on the move

Making a step in life is quite the dream of everyone, yet even with such hopes, we still fail to do so and get defeated in making such steps that move us forward towards our success. The difference with the individuals who succeed is that they are always on the move. They keep trying. To pursue excellence, we have to keep moving just like a river that wades through the obstacles that comes its way. Whether tough or simple, we have to keep on moving.

Without any reasonable doubt, success seems to be connected with action. Successful people keep on moving. They frequently make mistakes just like anyone of us. However, they never quit, and neither do they loose hope or even give up. Their lives are a true reflection of a fighting spirit. The never give up attitude makes them be on the move. To pursue excellence, we must never dwell in what is wrong yet rather focus on what to do next. To be on the move, we must spend our energies on moving forward towards finding possible appropriate solutions to our worries. A sure thing is that when we keep moving forward, we open new doors, find new opportunities and engage in doing new things since we are curious, and the curiosity keeps leading us down new paths.

Most times in life when encountered with panic and anxiety, we tend to let the conditions take over us. One thing we always fail to realize and acknowledge is the fact that, "life is not how it is supposed to be. It is the way it is. The way we cope with it, is that which makes the difference." When our lives are tied up with life obstacles, we ought not to worry. We ought to ensure we living limitless lives. We ought to be prepared to tackle these obstacles as they come on our way and keep on moving. One of my driving force to always be on the move is the fact that we need to always be on the run whenever flying becomes a difficult task, or walk if we can't run, crawl if we can't walk and if that isn't possible, then slither." All in all, whatever the circumstance, we need to be on the move. We have to keep moving towards our goals. It is generally difficult to make steps when things are in a comma but in every way, we have to keep on moving.

It's not until we make a personal decision to move forward that we begin making steps in life. Joel Osteen says, "We have to make a decision to move on, since it will never happen automatically. We will have to rise up and say,' I don't care how hard this is, I don't care how disappointed I am, I am not going to let this get the best of me. I am going to move on with my life."

Being on the move is anyway not any easy. Someone once quoted, "when the going gets tough, the tough get going." It's as simple as that. The expression may have been spoken by, Joseph P. Kennedy, the father to the late American President John F. Kennedy. The strong and tough individuals find this as a motivation to work harder and smarter when facing a challenge. Being on the move is a recipe of living a life without limits and requires us to press on, hold our head up and push harder.

To transition:

❖ Dwell in positivity

To be on the move, you got to surround yourself with positivity and not positive people. We must surround ourselves with positive things. The positive things can include people, surroundings, books and entertainment. All you got to strive to be to remain in a positive space. Negative people would breed negative thoughts and this would translate into our actions.

❖ Disregard the past

I know the fact that our pasts are the stepping stones to our future. Yet, it's our pasts that also stop us from moving to our future. To be on the move, one has to disregard his past, so that it doesn't stop him from achieving excellence. Life without limits acknowledges the fact that one has to accept that his past is real, but disregards the analogy that it the past should stop us from moving forward. More so, to be on the move, one has to take the necessary steps to deal with his past in a manner that it stops being a hindrance to his future.

Whereas life without limits underscores the fact that the past is important, it shouldn't turn to be a problem. Apostle Paul advises that we need to learn to forget and put our past behind us and then reach for things which are ahead. He says and I quote, "forgetting about those things which are behind and reaching to those things which are ahead, I press towards the goal for the prize of the upward call of God in Christ Jesus." (Philippians 3:13-14).

Believe you me. At times the past successes keep us rising to greater heights just as much as the past failures, but if we don't let go the old and embrace the new, then we all doomed. It really never matters what has happened in your history, but you got to let go the past and continue moving forward. 2nd Corinthians 5:17 says, "Behold the old has gone and the new has to come." True to it, even though we can't go back and make a brand new start, anyone can start from new and make a brand new ending as Carl Bard says. Disregard the past and focus ahead to be on the move. Life without limits awaits you ahead.

1. Recognize the power of dreaming in your life

The power of dreaming has driven personalities to where they are. Look at Joseph rising to the position of being a Prime Minister by just interpreting the Kings' dream.

Genesis 41:14-41 New International Version (NIV)

[14] So Pharaoh sent for Joseph, and he was quickly brought from the dungeon. When he had shaved and changed his clothes, he came before Pharaoh.
[15] Pharaoh said to Joseph, "I had a dream, and no one can interpret it. But I have heard it said of you that when you hear a dream you can interpret it."
[16] "I cannot do it," Joseph replied to Pharaoh, "but God will give Pharaoh the answer he desires."
[17] Then Pharaoh said to Joseph, "In my dream I was standing on the bank of the Nile, [18] when out of the river there came up seven cows, fat and sleek, and they grazed among the reeds. [19] After them, seven

other cows came up—scrawny and very ugly and lean. I had never seen such ugly cows in all the land of Egypt. 20 The lean, ugly cows ate up the seven fat cows that came up first. 21 But even after they ate them, no one could tell that they had done so; they looked just as ugly as before. Then I woke up.

22 "In my dream I saw seven heads of grain, full and good, growing on a single stalk. 23 After them, seven other heads sprouted—withered and thin and scorched by the east wind. 24 The thin heads of grain swallowed up the seven good heads. I told this to the magicians, but none of them could explain it to me."

25 Then Joseph said to Pharaoh, "The dreams of Pharaoh are one and the same. God has revealed to Pharaoh what he is about to do. 26 The seven good cows are seven years, and the seven good heads of grain are seven years; it is one and the same dream. 27 The seven lean, ugly cows that came up afterward are seven years, and so are the seven worthless heads of grain scorched by the east wind: They are seven years of famine.

28 "It is just as I said to Pharaoh: God has shown Pharaoh what he is about to do. 29 Seven years of great abundance are coming throughout the land of Egypt, 30 but seven years of famine will follow them. Then all the abundance in Egypt will be forgotten, and the famine will ravage the land. 31 The abundance in the

land will not be remembered, because the famine that follows it will be so severe. 32 The reason the dream was given to Pharaoh in two forms is that the matter has been firmly decided by God, and God will do it soon.

33 "And now let Pharaoh look for a discerning and wise man and put him in charge of the land of Egypt. 34 Let Pharaoh appoint commissioners over the land to take a fifth of the harvest of Egypt during the seven years of abundance. 35 They should collect all the food of these good years that are coming and store up the grain under the authority of Pharaoh, to be kept in the cities for food. 36 This food should be held in reserve for the country, to be used during the seven years of famine that will come upon Egypt, so that the country may not be ruined by the famine."

37 The plan seemed good to Pharaoh and to all his officials. 38 So Pharaoh asked them, "Can we find anyone like this man, one in whom is the spirit of God[a]?"

39 Then Pharaoh said to Joseph, "Since God has made all this known to you, there is no one so discerning and wise as you. 40 You shall be in charge of my palace, and all my people are to submit to your orders. Only with respect to the throne will I be greater than you."

Joseph in Charge of Egypt

41 So Pharaoh said to Joseph, "I hereby put you in charge of the whole land of Egypt."

Joseph's interpretations of the king's dream guaranteed him a position in the Land of Egypt. Despite being sold by his brothers, he had to move on. When one dreams big, he works hard towards achieving this dream. What follows is destiny and fate which moves in and the rest becomes history. Dreams are not a respecter of persons. They know no age. They know no gender, they know no race. Dare to dream. Your dreams have the ability to take you to the top.

It takes the same energy to dream big dreams and the same energy to dream small dreams. Someone says, "If dreams ain't waking you up, then it means you dreaming too small." To live a life without limits, you got to dream big and be on the move. Small dreams will take you nowhere. Dream big and be on the move. A life without limits awaits you. Greatness is a function of great dreams. By reading stories of great men and women, one realizes they all carry within them a life and world changing dreams. All you got to remember are these words, "if a man does not keep pace with his companions, perhaps it is because he's got a different drummer. Let him step to the music which he hears, however near or far away." Be on the move my brother and sister. Life without limits awaits you ahead.

CHAPTER NUGGETS

❖ Dreams are not a respecter of persons

❖ Greatness is a function of great dreams.

❖ To be on the move, you got to surround yourself
with positivity and not positive people.

❖ It takes the same energy to dream big dreams and
the same energy to dream small dreams.

* * * *

CHAPTER 9

BEYOND THE EXPECTATIONS

"When a man puts a limit on what he can do, he puts a limit on the far he goes."

Beyond the expectations

We're given birth to and raised in a world full of expectations. The prospects are so diverse such that: every member of the society has his or her own expectations of an individual. The moments you fail to reach these expectations as they perceive, then you are branded a failure and one ends up walking with the tag, "A failure" without realizing.

Humans' expectations are to a large extent shaped by the society and its culture. Our upbringing and our culture, including the media are powerful pigeonhole creators. Suppose I'm brought up believing that all politicians are uncaring rich people, that housewives and stay at home mums are lazy, that working moms are neglectful and that all that men care for are about power and sex then these stereotypes undoubtedly shape my expectations. Nevertheless, it's not just how we view others. The messages we receive impact how we see ourselves too.

Growing up, it was the desire of my parents to see me grow into a respectful, caring young man and who could take on his responsibilities. As a believer and a devoted

Christian, I trusted in God to see me through my life. I had desired to grow like the baby Jesus; in wisdom, in stature and in favor with God and man.

Expectations had defined my life and the year 2013 changed every aspect of my life in a way. The year had been one of my best having joined university for my campus education. Nevertheless, while I was celebrating the strides I had taken this far, the devil was busy trying to fix up his lies.

Fast forward, during this year, my life took a different turn from that which I had. My life had been robbed of the good health it enjoyed and sickness had taken a toll my life. Living alone then, I kept fighting for my dear life until the time it became unbearable. Being in the hospital bed, had for sure never been my cup of tea and never was it going to be. I for sure never imagined waking up in a hospital bed.

The semester had just come to an end and I travelled home for my vacations. During the holidays, I visited the hospital to have myself checked and this was seriously done. After a series of tests and scans, my family doctor briefed me of the findings and this was just unimaginable. For a while, I couldn't believe the doctor when he said I was suffering from Rheumatoid Arthritis. I had for a long time known that such diseases affect only the old and sure this was a time I had to change my thinking.

For a moment, I lost myself in thoughts and after sometime, I came back to my senses. I had a number of drugs to take. Surprisingly, in the doctors' record, he had diagnosed Arthritis back in 2012. This seemed a reality in the doctor's records but a fallacy in my mind. The holidays came to a close and I travelled back to school; several kilometers away from home. Surprisingly, as time progressed, the disease as well progressed. With time, my body organs got affected and there I was; writhing in pain in my body joints. Besides, the synovial fluid was seemingly getting done and at some points as I walked, I could get the knee bones knock.

This got worse and with time, I moved in to my elder brother's place. He did all he could to have me receive treatment. Friends came through and after a short while, I received a hospital referral to the Kenyatta Referral Hospital, for further treatment. I sure looked pale and even the nurses sympathized with my condition. After seeing a doctor, I was referred to a bone specialist and after a series of test, the results were the same; Rheumatoid Arthritis. Reality was now dawning on me and for sure, I had to live on drugs and on painkillers. The doc passed me an appointment in two weeks' time which I had to honor later on after taking my drugs.

The drugs were so expensive and I was worried how this was going to get along on. A number of friends sympathized with my condition. I ignored them and kept hope alive. Faith founded the basis of my life and all I hoped for was a complete healing once I finished the medication. Barely two weeks late, I could not even make it to school for my lectures. The pain was so severe. My joints and tissues were deeply in pain and could swell ocassionally.it was barely impossible to straighten my fingers and close my fists. All my joints ached. I would spend days at home in bed since I was unable to walk up or down the stairs, let alone walk to bus stage. My brother watched as all these unfolded and as I writhed in pain, he could at times watch helplessly.

The days turned into night and night into days and weeks later, I visited back the hospital for my routine checkups. Smiles were all people could see on my face, but deep within me, I was writhing in pain. My appointment time came and I walked in to see the doctor. A number of tests were done. So expensive were they that I began imagining of what life was going to be like if this is what I had to contend with. I was put on medications that eased the symptoms and pain for a short period of time, but then things were getting worse. I couldn't walk long distances then. I was fatigued all the time, and just the thought of having to walk to school some days made me shed tears. My feet's palm itched throughout the night and all I could do was scratching them through the night. This taught me a lesson...a lesson of perseverance....doing whatever I could to ease the discomfort. This taught me of how the many other things we take for granted were difficult or impossible for me to manage on my own from showering myself, getting to the shop or even cooking for myself and friends. I had to cut down on my class attendance from the normal 21 hours per week to just about 8 hours per week and even that was difficult to maintain because of the fatigued and the pain.

Two weeks before this, I was seated at the same position as I sat now and this time round, I believed the doctor was going to have a good report for me. I made a prayer as I waited for the tests results. For a moment, the doctor looked at me and when the moment came, he cleared his voice, "you have arthritis and I can confirm this again. The condition is called spondylo-arthritis." For a moment, I couldn't just get what he said and I sought clarification. "Your condition is advancing and I'd like you to go read about spondylo-arthritis." He stated. I was getting nervous and in within, I was burning.

I sat quietly in the medical room and after a moment I asked the doctor if this would be controlled and if id heal. "I'm sorry. This can only be controlled by taking strong painkillers, but it's a condition you will live with till death." In a quick rejoinder I said, "I am not going to die. I will live."

> *"This was a death sentence," I thought.*

"**This was a death sentence,**" I thought. I walked out of the office so dejected, but sure that it wasn't going to be a death sentence as decried. I spent lots of time reading about Arthritis. I got more and more depressed and really thought my life was over. This experience gave me a lesson to learn. I felt written off and weeks after weeks, I became weak and weaker. It was August, my best month; my birthday month. I grew so weak and for a while lost hope. I was going to die.

I couldn't speak then and could only communicate by writing. I had spoken to dad over the phone and tried to communicate as I murmured the words and which he couldn't grasp well. The communication wasn't just effective and after a while that night, I wrote a short message to my dad, "See you tomorrow." Very early the

next day, my young sister, Becky, took me to the bus stage
and I set for home, not really to see dad or mum or to heal
but to die while at home. After eight hours of travel, I
arrived home. Dad looked surprised and kept quiet for a
while then retreated to his restroom. He had been hit so
hard by my condition and it wasn't really what he thought it
to be. I really don't know why he never uttered a word but
got to his room. Not sure enough, but having known him, I
know he had gone to pray. My life had taken a turn from the
jolly young man I was to a different one today. I watched my
life turn from that of an Active young man in his early 20s to
a feeling and functioning like I was in my 60s or 70s in less
than an eight month frame. This was difficult to handle.

The days seemed longer and the nights were just the
longest. In bed, I lay the whole day and night and I cried a
number of times as I writhed in pain... Mum took a
compulsory leave from work for the entire period I was on
bed and she sincerely took care of me. She cooked my
meals, bathed me regularly; I remember her use a soft piece
of towel to clean me every two minutes. During the nights,
dad visited my room oftenly. I was in so much pain. I
literally cried and dad stood by the bed and prayed with me.
During the entire period, my dad and mum taught me to live
beyond people's expectations. I learnt to live beyond the
words of the doctor and I believed God. He was sure

working out things. Back at home, the doctors came to the house to treat me and for a while I was to be taken to the theatre room but instead I opted to believe in God. I declined to visit the hospital at all. I never went to the hospital any day and my nurse, Sis. Grace came to check on me in the morning, midday and evening. Her words always inspired me to move beyond the expectations. She kept motivating me and I had a reason to live. She sure always made me smile regardless of the pain I was undergoing. Her smile always gave me hope to live to see the next day and daily she ensured I smiled before she left. Thank you so much my nurse, Sister Grace Ontari, (The CCC In-charge, Homa-Bay County Teaching and Referral Hospital (HBCTRH). May God bless you for your dedication and compassion that's unprescribed.

Destined for greatness

I hadn't called off my school due to my ailment. For this reason, I had to travel back to undertake my end of semester exams without even attending the lectures. I had not planned to call off the semester to sit special exams and I had never hoped to ever sit special exams in my lifetime. I made arrangements and in mid- September, I travelled back to school. Mum was weary about my condition but I was upbeat about myself. It was sure going to be ten days of God's favor upon my life. I was certain he was going to watch over me. After a short talk and struggle, I convinced mum and she let me go.

God watched over me and my condition was controlled for the time I had my papers. I woke up, thanked God, took drugs and went to sit my papers. He was sure faithful. After the ten days, I travelled back home to complete my medication at the watch of my nurse, Sister Grace. I completed my dosage and went for the next ones.

The new semester began and I was well. I attended lectures but once again on the way, I felt things were not working in my favor. My health began deteriorating. I had begun to react to the drugs I was taking. They contained Sulphur and this was affecting me; my digestive tract, my breathing system. The drugs were really expensive and I spent much to visit the hospital every fortnight. We entrusted God to provide for my fees and my siblings school fees and for my medication and grandma at home. At some point, I felt the burden was much on my parents and elder brother who at time chipped in to facilitate my treatment. As a resolve, I decided to stop taking the drugs on my own.

None of my parents or siblings could understand the reason behind this move. I stopped taking medications to relieve my parents of the burden and I believed it was going to be time to completely trust God for a complete healing.

At this time, I had decided to live in accordance to the scripture that the Lord had revealed to me. This one night, the 26th July, 2013 at about 2a.m, I had severe pains that I could barely not sleep. I was at my elder brothers' residence and when I woke up; I had been sweating and had high fever. I took a cold shower despite the cold weather and sat at the couch. While seating at the couch, I made a short prayer and during this time, a voice called on unto me and instructed me to read the book of Jeremiah 30:17…… "…for I will restore health to you and heal you of your wounds. Says the Lord…" this verse formed the basis of my living from that day and to date it shapes my belief in a good health as a guarantee from the Almighty God. Verily, since stopping my medication, I have never regretted the decision. Very fortunately for me, my condition has continued to improve. Today, I am symptom free.

Your life, today, and tomorrow are gifts. Live your life without regrets. Learn from your past. Learn from your mistakes, and don't ever wish to have done anything differently. Everything that has happened, happens for a reason, it gets you to where you are today.

Love with every ounce of your soul, if you give that kind of love, someone, somewhere will want to give it back to you. Giving that kind of love and getting it in return, are an unparalleled experience. Enjoy life and all it has to offer. Enjoy your friends and family (even the annoying ones), sightsee and look at nature. Do what makes you happy; don't just talk about it- DO IT!

Be grateful for all these gifts- your life, your today and even tomorrow. Having the disease can be difficult. I'm not going to lie and say that's its easy. However, with the right doctors, the right medical team, the right support, the right attitude and trust in God, it is manageable.

Two months later after my end semester exams, results were out. Amazingly, I had not attended about 85 percent of my lectures. Nevertheless, my God was faithful. He for sure worked things out for me. My performance was sterling than even the previous ones. Destiny had taken its part. It sure wasn't a matter of chance but Choice.

CHAPTER NUGGETS

❖ Your life, today, and tomorrow are gifts. Live your life

without regrets. Learn from your past. Learn from your

mistakes, and don't ever wish to have done anything

differently. Everything that has happened, happens for a

reason, it gets you to where you are today.

* * * *

Morris J. Cerullo

CHAPTER 10

REPOSITION YOURSELF

Dare to wake up and achieve your dream. Dare to win.
You were made a winner from the beginning. Be the real you.

Living life without limits

Like a butterfly emerging from its own cocoon, you must discard the useless husk that you continue to cling around your dreams.

There are No limits:

All the limitations in our lives are self-imposed and we can overcome them. The one belief that will make you go beyond any limits is the belief that there are no limits. People without limits live in a continual state of curiosity. Curiosity is what causes us to learn and people without limits never stop learning. Remember during childhood periods how fascinating the world around us was. We always had a desire to know more. When we asked why we got the answer "because." If we asked why more than a number of times, there were dire consequences. But that very thing we were asked to stop doing, is the very thing that we did. That which we were stopped from doing was the very display of one of our limitless qualities.

Trying to please everybody is going to be a guaranteed waste of time. Allow me draw my inference from the Bible in regards to positioning of oneself.

"Now the Lord had said to Abram, get thee out of
thy country and from thy kindred, and from thy fathers
house, unto a land that I will show thee."
Genesis 12:1 (KJV).

Abraham would have died without being the faith of faith

By sharing the best of you with others, you discover the meaning and purpose of your existence. When you give and share the best of you with the world, you are at peace, you are content with yourself, your life and how things are in fact starting to attract in your life all that is needed, because you see, "everyone has a purpose in life...a unique one to themselves. Wayne Dyer alludes to this fact when he states that "I have absolutely no limits on what I intent to create."

Going to High school was my ultimate goal while in primary. I had learnt more about the upper learning institutions. My elder brother was already in high school and I had desired to follow in his footsteps. He had joined one of the top performing schools in the country and I had no option but to follow after him. Time was ripe and I had to join high school. I as well joined a top school in the nation but nearby due to certain national issues that weren't going to favor me join a school far away.

Joining high school, I had to make friends and sure I did. I met both tall and short people as well as people from both the urban areas and rural areas. One of those I met and have never forgotten is this young man, Nelson Odhiambo Okuto. We were admitted to the same stream in form one but to different dormitories. We had worked out our friendship together and a year down the line, we were involved in lots of activities together. We were one of the short form ones then and very quiet. We had become a darling of the teachers and most of the school officials. A year down the line, there was a reshuffle that was being done and fortunately enough, both of us were sent to a different stream from the one we were in. life wasn't going to be easy then but we forged to go on. A number of times, we skived together and went back to our previous class during the biology lessons due to our love for our form one biology teacher who was still teaching the stream we previously were in.

Despite the academics and co-curricular activities, we both were members of the Christian union which we had devoted ourselves to. It was during these meetings that we had strengthened our friendship since we seemed to have been driving the same agenda. Life at the school was at times not welcoming but we decided to forge ahead together. I remember attending a number of camp meetings during vacations together and we all encouraged ourselves to continue with or belief in God.

Coming from humble backgrounds, we had devoted ourselves to purse excellence to change the state of our lives.

Launch into the deep

We live in a world characterized by success and failure. A world characterized by great achievement and great transformations. A world where dreams are being fulfilled daily. Yet in the wake of all this, a number of us fail to discover their potential. As a result, they live in a world where there is no excuse for failure. Really though, as extraordinary great people discover their potentials and maximize on them, ordinary people fail to discover themselves and their capabilities. In a nutshell, great people never retire; they re-fire; that is they reignite their potentials. This keeps them going. They launch into the deep.

Excellence is available for you today. Go for it. Dare to wake up and achieve your dream. Dare to win. You were made a winner from the beginning. Be the real you. Don't be a hypocrite. If anyone can win, you can. If anyone deserves to be a change, you can. If anyone desires to fulfill his destiny, you surely can.

All you need is the Right Positioning.

CHAPTER NUGGETS

❖ All the limitations in our lives are self-imposed and we can overcome them

❖ By sharing the best of you with others, you discover the meaning and purpose of your existence.

❖ Be the real you. Don't be a hypocrite. If anyone can win, you can.

* * *

CHAPTER 11

LIVING ABOVE YOUR CIRCUMSTANCES

*"Tune Your Mind to the Positive, and look at life
from a different lens- a Godly lens."*

The Power of Perspective

L ife is not fair, it is never fair and neither shall it be fair. A child is brought to the fore and educated all the way to the university but fails to get himself or herself a job. Really life ain't fair. a mother carries a child with a hope of giving birth after nine months, but down the line after four months or so, she's informed of an ectopic pregnancy and loses the infant....life really ain't fair. Despite the challenges in life, one can still reposition himself or herself and achieve greatness. All you really need to do is to rise to the occasion and pursue your life goals.

Renewal of mind

And be not conformed to the patterns of this world:
but be you transformed by the renewing of your mind
that you may prove what is that good, and acceptable,
and perfect, will of God.
Romans 12:2 (KJV)

The mind is a very important organ.

A number of us today, are of the school of thought that the biggest problem the human mind contends with is the lack of knowledge it needs. They therefore are made to believe that, education becomes the greatest and only instrument of redemption — personal and social. Sited alone, I ponder on this and tend to think that if people just got more education, they would not use their minds to invent elaborate scams, and sophisticated terrorist plots, and complex schemes for embezzling, and fast-talking, mentally nimble radio rudeness. If people just got more education!

The mind holds with it lots of information. For sure, the problem with or minds today, is not merely that they are finite and lack information. The problem is that or minds are polluted. They are fallen. They possess a spirit, a bent mindset that is hostile to the absolute supremacy of God. People's minds are bent on not seeing positive things. Our minds are bent on not seeing God as infinitely more worthy of praise than we are, or the things *we* make or achieve.

This is what is acknowledged in Romans 1:28, "Since they did not see fit to acknowledge God, God gave them up to a debased mind." This is who we are by nature. We do not want to see God as worthy of knowing well and treasuring above all things. You know this is true about yourself because of how little effort you expend to know him, and because of how much effort it takes to make your mind spend any time getting to know God better. The Bible says we have "exchanged the glory of the immortal God for images resembling mortal man" (Romans 1:23). And the image in the mirror is the mortal image we worship most.

To attain the level of excellence you desire, you must position yourself to live beyond your circumstances. Just as one who wants to receive a blessing positions himself for a blessing, one has to position himself for excellence. To achieve excellence, we have to start on a journey to live beyond the limits of the world by seeing beyond our circumstances. Our circumstances at times hinder us from achieving excellence as we dwell on them so much to see the successes beyond them. All you need is to position yourself for excellence. It's not that you need to wait for God to decide to bless you. God wants you to be at your best. God will make you excel, if you position yourself for excellence. It all begins with the renewal of the mind.

MY FAITH UNRAVELLED

*Now faith is the substance of things hoped
for, the evidence of things not seen.
Hebrews 11:1 (NKJV)*

My friend, Erick A., through one of his Facebook posts, derives an in-depth description of what faith is. I totally consent to his school of thought of what faith is. He says, "Now faith is the confidence...being certain of change hoped for, speaking of the things that aren't seen as though they are."

Working for the public sector is the dream of every young man or woman. Many are made to believe that it's an easy-walk in the path working for the government. I was successful to acquire a place for my attachment at a public government Institution. This was a requirement for the partial fulfilment of my degree course and so had to attend an attachment program. Having secured a position for attachment with one of the devolved units in the Nation, I was upbeat that the skills acquired could be enormous and that I would easily get absorbed into the system by the HR department God willing. I attended to my duties faithfully and was so religious attending my attachment program. I made friends quickly as expected of me; both old and young, male and female.

With time, my attachment period came to an end and I had to depart. God favoured me and I soon became a darling to many at my workplace, that my boss even asked me to stay back and assist. I diligently carried on with my work and helped without showing any favouritism. Like Baby Jesus, God had granted me favour with my boss and colleagues and no amount of intimidation and or falsehood would see me sent parking. While working there, I learnt how sad it was that tribalism had entrenched even the workplace. The work politics had taken a toll. Tribalism just like in the national politics had since become one of the defining factors at my workplace and being so close to my boss, a number of his colleagues felt unsafe. I was soon being sent away. The murmurs were so loud. Yet, having a God-father who wasn't human, I was certain that he was preparing a table before my enemies. Surely, God worketh for the good of them who love the Lord. I escaped numerous traps set aside for me and really God was good.

Time fled, and one year down the line; I was still attached to my boss at the same organization. Allegations kept coming, one after the other, but the Almighty God preserved my life. One Wednesday afternoon, as I was going through my daily routine, I received a call from one of the senior officers concerning the loss of important office document. It was surprising to have myself linked to the loss of documents that I was never in possession over. I had never thought of such serious allegations being levelled against me and I thought for a moment this was an abuse of my good reputation. I prayed and asked God to see me through. I was summoned for interrogation. Barely an hour later after confrontations with the officers, God came through and I was released.

Fortunately, the situation was an eye opener. I began to realize how at times life presents difficult circumstances; some of which we can't even determine their onset, but really what action one takes makes the difference. You can always choose to be part of the mess or make a change.

Discouragement always sets in when one begins to feel hopeless about the future. However, looking beyond the circumstances to God, one is able to break forth and discover real hope and better future that is promised of us. Remember in Jeremiah 29:11 He says, "For I know the plans I have for you, plans for a future and a hope." Christ has good plans for us that guarantees us good future. Despite your stale marriage or chronic condition, there is a way- seek God and look beyond the circumstances. Ask God to open your eyes spiritually so you'll be able to see your circumstances from His perspective. Tune Your Mind to the Positive, and look at life from a different lens- a Godly lens that sees everything as possible and sees a bright future. By reciting this prayer, you can shift your perspective:

Loving Father, today, I seek to have an optimistic view on life. I seek to see opportunity in every situation and accept diverse and new ideas and viewpoints. I believe that all is working for the good of myself in you Lord. Help me through the renewal of my mind and this day, I accept to have an optimistic view on life. Amen

CHAPTER NUGGETS

❖ Life is not fair, it is never fair and neither shall it be fair. To attain the level of excellence you desire, you must position yourself to live beyond your circumstances.

❖ Tune Your Mind to the Positive, and look at life from a different lens- a Godly lens that sees everything as possible and sees a bright future.

CHAPTER 12

LET GO THE HEAVY BURDENS

"Accept (your) lot and be happy...this is a gift of God." You can take (Godly!) pride in relying on Christ with your load in life."
Ecclesiastes 5:19

<u>YOU DON'T HAVE TO CARRY HEAVY BURDENS</u>

There's a song best known to all of us. The song, 'Burdens are lifted at Calvary, Jesus is very near" is a song that speaks unto the deepest of our hearts on the need to lay our burdens at the cross. The song forms the basis of one of my best written articles in my **Lifespring Inspirations** webpage entitled, "*Donkeys don't carry heavy burdens...but they carry them anyway.*" One thing I'm certain about is the fact that most of us believe that donkeys are meant to carry heavy burdens. I really don't know what shapes the thinking. Probably it's because donkeys' lives are always characterized by carrying of heavy stuffs. Yet my thinking is from a different perspective and this is what I write on the webpage.

Born of strong bones, thick of hide and obstinate of mind. They are probably regarded the most hardworking domesticated creatures. Born into the service of a human master, the master places heavy loads on its back without a complaint or even a second thought. He stands there and continues munching the grass. A man walks by and laments how stubborn the animal is and what follows is a whip and beatings. Without a complaint, the donkey digs his heel deeper into the earth and refuses to budge. What a creation.

The master's neighbor and friend walks by and says, "Your beast needs to be taught his purpose. He's got a burden that's too light- so he thinks all that's required of him is munching grass." They bring in more goods and foodstuffs to increase the donkey's load. What follows is the collapse of the donkey. Indeed donkeys do not carry heavy burdens .... but they carry them anyway.

Walking in the streets, one comes across people of diverse backgrounds. One unfortunate thing is that some of these people live hopeless lives coupled with lots of desperation and heart breaks. They keep lamenting how deep down their hearts they got loads of burdens; some of which are self-inflicted. Another group sobs from the burdens they carry. But under all these circumstances, the most unfortunate thing is that most times we neglect our loads and turn them into burdens. We force our loads into unnecessary burdens that translates into a stumbling block. Even though, the Bible calls us to bear each other's burden (Galatians 6:2), we must distinguish between carrying one another's' burden or enabling them. Carrying self-imposed burdens impact negatively on our lives and often lead to one's collapse.

Maybe we find ourselves in such situations, having oppressive, crushing weight that outweighs us even when we try to shake it. And while under the influence of powerful stimulants and emotions, we seem to have periods where there seems to be relief. Yet in the quiet moments of reflection that inevitably come, we realize that we ain't living the life we yearn for. We even tie this burdens to spells cast against us and we feel that the Lord has abandoned us and so have friends. However, in moments of self-reflection, you realize it's you who has abandoned them. This hurts and ails. Even so there exists a solution...that is focusing on the cross. When life requires us to push harder, to protect more vigilantly, to give more freely, to expend unavailable energies, to accomplish impossible tasks, God offers us his sustaining love, his gentle concern, his guiding sovereignty.

He says in Ecclesiastes 5:19,

"Accept (your) lot and be happy...this is a gift of God." You can take (Godly!) pride in relying on Christ with your load in life.

If an overwhelming problem, sin or weakness is pressing you down, all you need is to be humble enough to say, Hey, I need someone to pray with me! This is too much for me to do completely by myself! It may be difficult for you to open your heart and reveal your need, but it will be far more difficult for you to carry it alone until you eventually become emotionally devastated by that burden. We don't have to burden our lives with heavy burdens lest we collapse. The cross offers us the opportunity to lay our burdens and proceed with a lighter weight. Forget about carrying other peoples' burdens over your load. Help them approach the cross where rest is guaranteed.

If we got to live a life without limits, we have to come to the realization that we ain't made to carry burdens. In fact, burdens are lifted at Calvary. They are lifted at the cross, where adequate rest is guaranteed. A number of times we carry burdens that make us live a life that's limiting. Going forth, you got to lift the burdens you got at the cross...

If we got to live a life without limits, we have to come to the realization that we aren't made to carry burdens. In fact, burdens are lifted at Calvary. They are lifted at the cross where rest is guaranteed.

Morris Cerullo

CHAPTER NUGGETS

❖ Donkeys don't carry heavy burdens…but they carry them anyway."

❖ Burdens are lifted at Calvary. They are lifted at the cross, where adequate rest is guaranteed.

* * *

CHAPTER 13

RECOGNIZING THE POWER OF

PRAYER

"The effectual fervent prayer of a righteous
man availeth much. "
James 5:16

The power of prayer

The power of prayers can never be underestimated in whichever level one is. One thing known to every mankind, whether saved or not is that prayer is a key that unlocks doors. Life was ordained by God when he breathed into the nostril of man at the beginning and that's an undisputed fact. The bible says in Genesis 2:7, "The Lord God formed the man from the dust of the ground and breathed into his nostrils the breath of life, and the man became a living creature." When God breathed into man's nostril, he breathed his intention of a limitless life into man. In this way, he breathed life. This is witnessed as the breath of life, turned man from a lifeless collection of matter into a living creature.

A while back in my early years of life, I had a mission to accomplish. My Dad being a minister of the Word was tasked to go plant a church together with other ministers. We were set to leave on Friday, a day after the other ministers had left for the town they were to plant the new church. I was very happy as always to accompany my dad to minister the word. He was set to minister this Friday afternoon at the New church. Early that morning, we set for this town about 85 kilometers away from our residential town. While on the bus, the conductor approached us requesting our bus fare. Unfortunately, my dad looked into his bag and pockets but couldn't find the amount he had. He looked into his wallet once again but there was no money. While still astonished, the driver was asked to stop the bus and we were thrown out of the bus. So embarrassing was this but we had no option but to walk out of the bus.

Fast forward, the only option left was walking back home, about 25 kilometers. I couldn't imagine walking this distance. I requested dad to once again check his bag. He only found thirty shilling coin. We needed at least fifty shillings to get home. It was dawning on me that we had to walk. We prayed and began walking and a short while, a matatu came. We stopped it and got in. surprisingly, all that was needed from us was thirty shillings. After minutes later, we were home. Mum couldn't believe and so were my siblings. We explained everything and Dad set to his room to check if at all he had forgotten the bus fare. There was nothing. As the priest of the house, he asked us to join in prayers. We all retreated to our rooms and prayed. At about 12 noon, mum prepared a meal and we ate. The next bus was leaving at 1pm. We got ready for this journey all without bus fare. Dad was to be ministering at 2pm. He hadn't cancelled his going. After our meal, dad retreated to his room once again. This time round, he came back with a good report. Our prayers had been answered. He had found some money in one of his coats. We set once again for the journey and at 2.30pm, he was ministering.

I believe that this wasn't a case of being forgetful but a case of answered prayers. The bible acknowledges the power of effectual fervent prayers and the outcome to the righteous. To live a life without limits, then we have to soak ourselves in a prayer life. One has to Pray Until Something Happens (PUSH). When you begin recognizing the power of prayers then you begin getting into a path of living a life that was ordained by God. Jesus Christ often retreated to prayers before his ministry and even during his ministry. This ensured that he lived a life without limits. Just like a river wades off its way while dodging any obstacle it comes across so should our lives be. The river never stops its desire to reach the final destination from the source and that's just how our lives were designed by the chief designer. We were designed to live a limitless life but this can only be accomplished through continuous supplication unto the father who breathed the breath of life into our lives.

For sure the only reason as to why man is living a life that is limited is because we have sort permission to do so. We have decided to conform to patterns of this world. Come on, the bible commands us in Romans 12:2, not to conform to the patterns of this world. What mankind has done is to conform unto the different worldly patterns which are barring us from living the lives designed by the designer. One aspect we fail to realize is that when a product ceases to operate as designed by the designer, then it's done away with. This is what the bible says in John 15:1-2, "I am the true vine, my father is the gardener. He cuts off every branch in me that bears no fruit, while every branch that bears fruit he prunes so that it will be more fruitful." The moment we stop living our lives as designed by the designer, be rest assured that you are cut off.

One sure thing is that effectual fervent prayer of a righteous is able to make him live a life without limits. It is my desire that we all live the life designed by the chief designer. He indeed has good plans for each of us as declared in Jeremiah 29:11. Don't wait for tomorrow, you got to live the life without limits beginning NOW!

CHAPTER NUGGETS

❖ Life was ordained by God when he breathed into the nostril of man at the beginning and that's an undisputed fact.

❖ Effectual fervent prayer of a righteous man is able to make him live a life without limits

❖ When a product ceases to operate as designed by the designer, then it's done away with.

❖ The moment we stop living our lives as designed by the designer, be rest assured that you are cut off.

* * *

> **When you begin recognizing the power of prayers then you begin getting into a path of living a life that was ordained by God.**

CHAPTER 14

LIVING A LIFE WORTHY OF THE CALLING

"¹As a prisoner for the Lord, then, I urge you to live a life worthy of the calling you have received. ² Be completely humble and gentle; be patient, bearing with one another in love. ³ Make every effort to keep the unity of the Spirit through the bond of peace. ⁴ There is one body and one Spirit, just as you were called to one hope when you were called; ⁵ one Lord, one faith, one baptism; ⁶ one God and Father of all, who is over all and through all and in all."

Ephesians 4:1-6

Living a life worthy of your calling

Finally, brothers and sisters, I can continue writing and writing, yet wisdom informs me of the need to conclude in this chapter. This is what I'm called to be- an inspiration through my literary works, enabled by the Grace of God the Father. Even as I pen this last chapter of this book, I feel admonished, pushed and compelled to speak about living a life worthy of our calling as a key aspect of living life without limits.

As I read through the book for the final time before its publication, I am driven to the aspect of limits and boundaries. Could be you have been reading through the print book and you still wondering what it is to live a life without limits. You got not to worry brother or sister. I got you covered. Boundaries and limits are way two different terminologies. Their meanings are often blurred. In accordance to the dictionary, boundaries imply markings or points by which the limits are marked or established. They can be physical or not. Limits are restrictions or points where something does not or cannot extend or pass. From the definition, it is possible to conclude that limits are physical while boundaries ain't..

And so, What if we lived life without limits? Not without

boundaries, but without LIMITS!

Probably you may be questioning how it happened that we at times find ourselves living lives of confinement and limitation. Does it mean that there are insurmountable obstacles or burdens too heavy to carry? Or have we misunderstood God? Have we restricted the very lives that Jesus lived, died, and lives again to provide?

In the previous chapters I paint a view that in God's plan of action, his desire was to have man live a life not characterized by limits. Note the word limits and not boundaries. Man was to live a life without limits. He was to go beyond the limits of life to live a life worthy of his calling. But what really happened?

My elder brother, John Aggrey, was born asthmatic. At his younger age, he was too young to even understand why he had such a condition. He lived with this condition since birth that it had even become normal for him. It was now part of him. We had got accustomed to this and even knew all the precautions to take. In spite of his health condition, Aggrey played soccer, "his favorite game" and so bad that at times he played in cold weather. He knew his boundaries (stayed indoors during the cold and put on warm clothes) but knew no limits (still enjoyed playing his soccer game). The fact that he had scars never affected his life.

It's important to understand that we all have scars; both physical and emotional scars. However, we don't have to be limited by our scars and neither do we have to be limited by our fears. Today, John Aggrey ain't asthmatic and is a renowned soccer analyst. Scars and fears can stop us dead in our tracks, if we let them.

God has indeed granted us life beyond measure. Knowing that, wouldn't it stand to reason that our lives would be enlarged by His gift of life without limits? Wouldn't those around us be changed as well?

Paul makes a call to action. He reminds us of the greater calling that we attained by grace. Yet the reason why we are to life such a life is because we received a call into it. Walking, in itself, requires consistency. When we were born, walking never became an immediate skill; rather it is something we learned. This is true also in living a life without limits and also in the spiritual realm. Walking with God is a practical skill that takes time to learn. Living a life without limits takes time to learn. Once you learn to walk, then you get a lifetime to practice and keep form.

Friends, '**Life without Limits,**' is nothing different from living a life worthy of the calling. It is a life worthy of the gospel. The question today is; Are you living this life?

Prayer

Heavenly Father, May you grant us the grace to live a life that's worthy of our calling and the gospel of the cross. In Jesus Mighty name. Amen

CHAPTER NUGGETS

- ❖ God's plan of action, his desire was to have man live a life not characterized by limits

- ❖ We all have scars; both physical and emotional scars.

- ❖ Walking with God is a practical skill that takes time to learn. Living a life without limits takes time to learn.

Jeremiah 29:11

"For I know the thoughts and plans I have for you, says the Lord, thoughts and plans for welfare and peace and not for evil, to give you hope in your final outcome." (Amplified version)

<u>NOTES</u>

<u>NOTES</u>

REFERENCE BOOKS

1. THE HOLY BIBLE
2. AN ENEMY CALLED AVERAGE- JOHN L. MASON
3. CONQUERING AN ENEMY CALLED AVERAGE- JOHN L. MASON
4. IMITATION IS LIMITATION – JOHN L. MASON
5. THE POWER OF POSITIVE THINKING – NORMAN VINCENT PEALE
6. A-Z SECRETS OF HIGH ACHIEVERS- PST. ALFRED ARITA

Thanks to every reader

For Motivational and Mentorship programs, Life coaching forums, workshops, seminar.

Contact me on

TEL: +254 706 590 156 OR +254 737 818 739

EMAIL: morrispeterz@gmail.com OR Lifespring40@gmail.com

Https://Lifespring40.wordpress.com

Made in the USA
Columbia, SC
17 July 2022

63572895R00086